# Introduction:

Starting a business from home can be a great way to become your own boss and achieve financial independence. However, it can also be challenging and risky. This book will provide you with the knowledge and tools you need to start and grow a successful business from home.

Chapter 1: Assessing Your Business Idea

- Assessing the feasibility and profitability of your business idea
- Conducting market research to identify your target market and competitors
- Identifying the skills and resources you'll need to start and run your business

Chapter 2: Creating a Business Plan

- Developing a clear vision and mission statement
- Setting goals and objectives
- Creating a financial plan, including projected income and expenses
- Developing a marketing plan to promote your business

Chapter 3: Setting Up Your Business

- Registering your business and obtaining any necessary licenses and permits
- Setting up your business structure, whether it is a sole proprietorship, partnership, LLC or corporation
- Establishing a legal and tax compliance
- Setting up a business bank account

Chapter 4: Building and Managing Your Business

- Building and managing your online presence, including website, social media, and online marketplaces
- Managing your finances and accounting

- Building and managing a team
- Managing your inventory and supply chain

Chapter 5: Growing Your Business

- Identifying and taking advantage of new opportunities
- Utilizing digital marketing strategies to reach new customers
- Expanding your product or service offerings
- Building and maintaining relationships with customers, suppliers, and partners

Conclusion: Starting a business from home can be a rewarding experience, but it also requires dedication, hard work, and the right tools and strategies. By following the advice in this book, you'll be on your way to building a successful business from home. Remember to stay flexible and adapt to the changes in the market and the economy, and don't be afraid to ask for help when you need it. Good luck on your entrepreneurial journey!

# Introduction:

Starting a business from home is a dream for many entrepreneurs. The idea of being your own boss and working from the comfort of your own home can be incredibly appealing. However, starting a business from home also comes with its own set of unique challenges. From assessing the feasibility of your business idea to building an online presence and managing finances, there are a lot of moving parts to consider.

But the good news is, it can be done. With the right tools, knowledge, and strategies, you can start and grow a successful business from home. This book is here to guide you through the process, providing you with the information you need to make informed decisions and navigate the challenges that come with starting a business from home.

We'll start by assessing your business idea, conducting market research, and identifying the skills and resources you'll need to start and run your business. Next, we'll delve into creating a business plan and setting up your business legally and financially. We'll also cover how to build and manage your business, including creating an online presence and managing your finances and accounting.

Finally, we'll discuss how to grow your business, including identifying new opportunities, using digital marketing strategies to reach new customers, and building relationships with customers, suppliers, and partners.

This book is not only for the first-time entrepreneurs but also for those who are running their business from home for a while but are looking for new ways to expand, adapt to the market changes, and face the challenges that come with running a business from home. By following the advice in this book, you'll have the knowledge, tools, and strategies you need to start and grow a successful business from home.

So, whether you're looking to start a business from home or take your existing business to the next level, this book is your ultimate guide to success. Let's begin the journey of entrepreneurship together!

# Chapter 1: Assessing Your Business Idea

Starting a business from home can be an exciting and fulfilling endeavor, but it's important to make sure that your business idea is both feasible and profitable. Assessing the feasibility and profitability of your business idea is the first step in creating a solid foundation for your business.

## Assessing Feasibility

Feasibility refers to the ability of your business idea to be executed and sustained in the marketplace. Before you start your business, it's important to assess whether your idea is viable by considering factors such as the size of your target market, the competition, and the cost of starting and running your business.

One way to assess the feasibility of your business idea is to conduct a SWOT analysis. A SWOT analysis is a tool used to evaluate the strengths, weaknesses, opportunities, and threats of a business idea. By analyzing these factors, you can identify potential challenges and opportunities for your business, as well as areas where you may need to improve or adapt your business idea.

## Assessing Profitability

Profitability refers to the ability of your business to generate enough revenue to cover expenses and provide a profit. In order to be successful, your business must be able to generate enough revenue to cover the costs of starting and running your business, as well as provide a profit.

To assess the profitability of your business idea, you'll need to conduct market research. Market research is the process of gathering and analyzing information about your target market, competitors, and industry trends. By conducting market research, you can gain a better understanding of the size of your target market, your competitors, and the potential demand for your products or services.

# Conducting Market Research

Conducting market research is an important step in assessing the feasibility and profitability of your business idea. Market research can help you identify your target market, understand your competitors, and identify industry trends.

There are several different methods you can use to conduct market research, including:

- Surveys: Surveys are a great way to gather information from a large number of people in a relatively short amount of time. You can conduct surveys online or in person, and you can use a variety of survey tools, such as SurveyMonkey or Google Forms.
- Focus groups: Focus groups are a great way to gather qualitative data about your target market. You can conduct focus groups in person or online, and you can use a variety of tools, such as Zoom or Google Meet.
- Interviews: Interviews are a great way to gather information from a small number of people. You can conduct interviews in person or over the phone, and you can use a variety of tools, such as Skype or Google Voice.
- Online research: Online research is a great way to gather information about your target market, competitors, and industry trends. You can use a variety of tools, such as Google Analytics or SEMrush, to gather information about your competitors and industry trends.

## Identifying Skills and Resources

After assessing the feasibility and profitability of your business idea and conducting market research, the next step is to identify the skills and resources you'll need to start and run your business.

Identifying the skills and resources you'll need will help you to create a plan for acquiring them and also give you an idea of the cost of starting and running your business.

The skills and resources you'll need will vary depending on the type of business you're starting. Some common skills and resources you may need include:

- Business skills: skills in marketing, accounting, finance, and management
- Technical skills: skills in web development, graphic design, or programming
- Equipment: computers, smartphones, internet access, and office equipment
- Software: accounting software, customer relationship management software, and marketing automation software
- Physical space: a dedicated home office or workspace for your business
- Legal and regulatory compliance: knowledge of laws and regulations related to your business, such as taxes, permits, and licenses
- Funding: startup capital to cover the costs of starting and running your business

By identifying the skills and resources you'll need to start and run your business, you'll be able to create a plan for acquiring them and also have a better understanding of the cost of starting and running your business. It's also important to keep in mind that as your business grows, your skills and resources needs may change, so it's important to be flexible and adaptable.

In summary, assessing the feasibility and profitability of your business idea is an important first step in starting a successful business from home. By conducting market research, identifying your target market and competitors, and identifying the skills and resources you'll need, you'll be able to create a solid foundation for your business and increase your chances of success.

# Chapter 2: Creating a Business Plan

Creating a business plan is an essential step in starting a successful business from home. A business plan is a document that outlines the purpose and goals of your business, and it includes a detailed analysis of your target market, products and services, financial projections, and marketing strategies.

## Developing a Clear Vision and Mission Statement

The first step in creating a business plan is to develop a clear vision and mission statement. A vision statement is a long-term view of what you want to achieve with your business, while a mission statement defines the purpose of your business and how you plan to achieve that vision. A clear vision and mission statement will provide direction and focus for your business, and will help you to stay on track as you make decisions and set goals.

## Setting Goals and Objectives

Once you have a clear vision and mission statement, the next step is to set specific goals and objectives for your business. These should be measurable, attainable, relevant, and time-bound (SMART) goals that align with your vision and mission statement.

For example, you may set a goal to increase revenue by 20% within the next year, or to acquire a certain number of new customers within the next six months. Setting goals and objectives will help you to stay focused and motivated, and will provide a clear benchmark for measuring your progress.

## Creating a Financial Plan

Creating a financial plan is a critical step in starting a successful business from home. This includes projected income and expenses, as well as a cash flow forecast. It's important to be realistic and conservative when creating your financial plan, and to include contingencies for unexpected events. Your financial plan should also include a projected break-even point, which is the point at which your revenue will cover your expenses. This will help you to determine how much revenue you'll need to generate in order to become profitable.

## Developing a Marketing Plan

Developing a marketing plan is essential for promoting your business and reaching your target market. Your marketing plan should include a detailed analysis of your target market, as well as strategies for reaching them.

This may include tactics such as social media marketing, content marketing, email marketing, and search engine optimization (SEO). Your marketing plan should also include a budget and timelines for implementing your strategies.

In conclusion, creating a business plan is an essential step in starting a successful business from home. By developing a clear vision and mission statement, setting specific goals and objectives, creating a financial plan, and developing a marketing plan, you'll be able to create a roadmap for your business and stay on track as you move forward. A well-written business plan will also be useful if you plan to seek funding or investment for your business.

# Chapter 3: Setting Up Your Business

In order to start a successful business from home, there are several key steps you'll need to take to set up your business properly. This includes registering your business, obtaining any necessary licenses and permits, setting up your business structure, establishing legal and tax compliance, and setting up a business bank account. In this chapter, we will dive deeper into each of these steps to ensure that you have a comprehensive understanding of the process.

## Registering Your Business

The first step in setting up your business is to register it with the appropriate government agencies. This typically includes registering your business name and obtaining any necessary licenses and permits. The process for registering your business will vary depending on your location and the type of business you're starting, so it's important to research the specific requirements for your area. Some businesses may require additional licenses or permits, such as food service businesses or those that involve the use of hazardous materials.

When registering your business, it's important to choose a name that is unique and distinguishable from other businesses in your industry. This will help you to establish a strong brand identity and make it easier for customers to find and remember your business. In addition, you'll need to register for any necessary state and local taxes, such as sales tax and business personal property tax.

## Setting Up Your Business Structure

The next step in setting up your business is to choose the appropriate business structure. The most common options include sole proprietorship, partnership, LLC, or corporation. Each structure has its own advantages and disadvantages, so it's important to research and consider which one is the best fit for your business. A sole proprietorship is the simplest and least expensive option, while a corporation is more complex and expensive, but provides the most personal liability protection.

A sole proprietorship is the most basic business structure and is often the preferred choice for those who are just starting out. It is easy to set up and maintain, and there are few formalities to follow. However, it also has the disadvantage of unlimited personal liability, which means that the owner is personally responsible for all debts and liabilities of the business.

A partnership is similar to a sole proprietorship, but it involves two or more people. Partners share profits and losses and are jointly liable for the debts and liabilities of the business. This can be a good option for those who want to start a business with a partner or group of partners, but it does come with the added complexity of managing multiple relationships and decision-making processes.

A Limited Liability Company (LLC) is a hybrid business structure that combines the personal liability protection of a corporation with the tax benefits of a partnership. It is a more complex structure than a sole proprietorship or partnership, but it can provide more flexibility and protection for the business owners.

A corporation is a separate legal entity that is owned by shareholders. It provides the most personal liability protection for the owners, but it also involves the most complexity and expense. It is often chosen by businesses that plan to go public or raise significant capital.

# Establishing Legal and Tax Compliance

Once you've set up your business structure, it's important to establish legal and tax compliance. This includes obtaining any necessary federal and state tax IDs, registering for any required taxes, and obtaining any necessary insurance. It's also important to establish record-keeping procedures and to stay up-to-date on any changes in laws and regulations that may affect your business.

In addition to choosing a business structure, you will also need to establish legal and tax compliance. This will involve registering for any relevant taxes, such as sales tax or income tax, and obtaining any necessary insurance to protect your business and your personal assets. It is important to consult with a lawyer or other professional to ensure that you are complying with all relevant laws and regulations.

Finally, you will need to set up a business bank account. This will allow you to separate your personal finances from your business finances, making it easier to track your income and expenses and to apply for loans or other forms of financing. To open a business bank account, you will typically need to provide proof of your business registration and your tax ID number, as well as any other information required by the bank.

Setting up your business involves a number of important steps, including registering your business and obtaining any necessary licenses or permits, setting up your business structure, establishing legal and tax compliance, and setting up a business bank account. While the process can be complex, it is essential to ensure that your business is set up properly in order to be successful. Be sure to do your research and consult with a lawyer or other professional to ensure that you are complying with all relevant laws and regulations.

# Chapter 4: Building and Managing Your Business

Building and managing your online presence is crucial for the success of your home-based business. Your website is the foundation of your online presence and serves as a hub for all of your online activity.

## Building and Managing Your Online Presence

In today's digital age, having an online presence is crucial for the success of any business. Not only does it make it easier for customers to find and learn about your business, but it also allows you to reach a wider audience. When building and managing your online presence, there are several key elements to consider, including your website, social media, and online marketplaces.

## Website

Your website is the foundation of your online presence. It is the first point of contact for most potential customers and should be designed to provide a positive user experience. When building your website, consider the following:

- Use a professional design: Your website should be visually appealing and easy to navigate. Invest in a professional web designer or use a website builder to ensure your website looks polished and professional.

- Optimize for SEO: Search engine optimization (SEO) is the process of optimizing your website to rank higher in search engine results. Optimize your website for SEO by including keywords in your content, using meta tags, and building backlinks.

- Include important information: Your website should include important information about your business, such as your contact information, products or services, and pricing.

## Social Media

Social media is a powerful tool for building your brand and engaging with customers. Platforms such as Facebook, Twitter, and Instagram allow you to share updates, promotions, and other content with your followers. When building and managing your social media presence, consider the following:

- Choose the right platforms: Not all social media platforms are right for every business. Choose the platforms that are most popular among your target market and focus on building a presence on those.

- Create a content strategy: Develop a content strategy that includes a mix of promotional and educational content. This will help you to keep your followers engaged and informed about your business.

- Engage with your followers: Respond to comments and messages, and actively engage with your followers. This will help to build trust and loyalty among your customers.

## Online Marketplaces

Online marketplaces such as Amazon and Etsy allow you to sell your products or services to a wider audience. When building and managing your presence on online marketplaces, consider the following:

- Choose the right marketplace: Not all online marketplaces are right for every business. Choose the marketplace that is most popular among your target market and that offers the best opportunities for your products or services.

- Optimize your listing: Optimize your listing by including high-quality images, detailed product descriptions, and customer reviews. This will make your products more attractive to potential customers.

- Manage your inventory: Keep track of your inventory levels and restock as needed. This will help to ensure that you never run out of stock and can continue to meet customer demand.

Building and managing your online presence is essential for the success of your business. By developing a strong website, engaging on social media, and leveraging online marketplaces, you can reach a wider audience and increase your visibility. With the right strategy, you can build a strong online presence that will help to drive sales and growth for your business.

Managing your online presence can be time-consuming, but it is essential for the success of your business. By creating a professional and informative website, building a community on social media, and reaching new customers through online marketplaces, you can increase your visibility and build trust with potential customers. With the right approach and a bit of effort, you can create an online presence that will help your business thrive.

# Managing your finances and accounting

Managing your finances and accounting is one of the most critical aspects of running a successful business. Whether you're just starting out or have been in business for a while, it's essential to understand the financial side of your business and how to manage it effectively. In this chapter, we'll discuss the basics of financial management and accounting for your business, including how to create a budget, track your income and expenses, and make informed financial decisions.

One of the first things you'll need to do when setting up your business is to create a budget. A budget is a financial plan that outlines your income, expenses, and savings goals for a specific period of time. It's essential to have a budget in place so you can track your progress and make sure you're staying on track financially. The budget should be based on your projected income and expenses, and should be reviewed and updated regularly.

Another important aspect of financial management is tracking your income and expenses. This includes keeping accurate records of all the money coming in and going out of your business. You'll need to create a system for tracking your income and expenses, whether it's using software or a simple spreadsheet. This will help you understand where your money is going and identify any areas where you can cut costs or increase revenue.

Once you have a good handle on your income and expenses, you can start making informed financial decisions. This means analyzing your financial data and using it to make decisions about how to allocate your resources, invest in new opportunities, and manage risk. For example, if you see that your expenses are higher than your income, you'll need to take steps to reduce your costs or increase your revenue.

Managing your finances and accounting also includes managing your taxes. It's important to understand the tax laws and regulations that apply to your business, and to stay compliant with them. This includes keeping accurate records of your income and expenses, and filing your taxes on time. You'll also need to decide whether to hire an accountant or do your own accounting, depending on your business's size and complexity.

In summary, managing your finances and accounting is an essential aspect of running a successful business. By creating a budget, tracking your income and expenses, making informed financial decisions, and staying compliant with tax laws, you'll be able to manage your finances effectively and ensure the long-term success of your business.

## Building and managing a team

Managing a team is a critical aspect of any business, and even more so when running a business from home.

Building and managing a team can help you to achieve your business goals and objectives, and also help you to handle the day-to-day tasks that come with running a business.

When building and managing a team, it is important to identify the roles and responsibilities that need to be filled within your business. This will help you to determine the number of people you need to hire, and also help you to identify the skills and qualifications that you need in your team members.

One of the most important aspects of building and managing a team is communication.

It is essential to have clear and open lines of communication within your team to ensure that everyone is on the same page and that tasks are completed efficiently.

This can be achieved through regular team meetings, setting clear expectations, and providing regular feedback on performance.

Another important aspect of building and managing a team is setting clear goals and objectives. Having a shared understanding of what your team is working towards will help to keep everyone focused and motivated.

It is also important to establish a system of accountability within your team, so that everyone knows their role and is held responsible for their actions.

When it comes to managing your finances and accounting, it is important to keep accurate records of all financial transactions and to have a clear understanding of your financial position at all times.

This will help you to make informed decisions about how to manage your finances and to identify any areas where you may need to cut costs.

You should also create a budget for your business and stick to it as much as possible. This will help you to keep your expenses in check and to avoid overspending.

It is also important to keep track of your cash flow, so that you know when you will have money coming in and when you will need to pay bills.

In addition to keeping accurate records and creating a budget, it is also important to have a basic understanding of accounting principles and to stay up to date with any changes in tax laws that may affect your business. You may also want to consider hiring an accountant to help you with your finances and accounting.

Managing your inventory and supply chain is another important aspect of running a business from home. It is important to have a clear understanding of your inventory levels at all times, so that you can make informed decisions about when to restock and when to hold off on ordering more products. This can help you to avoid overstocking, which can be costly, and also help you to avoid running out of stock, which can result in lost sales.

You should also be aware of the lead times for your products, so that you can plan ahead and make sure that you always have enough stock on hand. This will help you to avoid stockouts and keep your customers happy.

It is also important to have a clear understanding of your supply chain and to establish good relationships with your suppliers. This will help you to ensure that you always have a steady supply of products and also help you to negotiate better prices and terms.

In conclusion, building and managing a team, managing your finances and accounting, and managing your inventory and supply chain are all critical aspects of running a successful business from home.

By understanding the importance of each of these areas and putting systems in place to manage them effectively, you can help to ensure the success of your business and achieve your goals and objectives.

## Managing Your Inventory and Supply Chain

An efficient inventory management system is crucial to the success of your business, regardless of the size of your operation or the products you sell. It can help you ensure that you always have the right products in stock, while reducing waste, controlling costs, and improving customer satisfaction.

A well-managed supply chain can also help you to maintain consistent quality, respond quickly to changes in demand, and reduce the risk of stockouts or overstocking.

Now, we will discuss the importance of inventory management and the steps you can take to build an effective supply chain.

Why is Inventory Management Important? Inventory management is important for several reasons, including:

- Controlling costs: By accurately tracking inventory levels, you can avoid overstocking, reduce waste, and minimize the risk of stockouts. This can help you to reduce costs and increase profitability.
- Improving customer satisfaction: A well-managed inventory system can help you to ensure that you always have the right products in stock, so you can meet customer demand and improve customer satisfaction.
- Maintaining quality: By monitoring inventory levels and quickly responding to changes in demand, you can maintain consistent quality and avoid the risk of stockouts or overstocking.
- Responding quickly to changes in demand: A good inventory management system can help you to quickly respond to changes in demand, which can help you to maintain profitability and improve customer satisfaction.

Building an Effective Supply Chain An effective supply chain starts with a clear understanding of your products, suppliers, and customers. Here are the steps you can take to build a supply chain that works for your business:

1. Define your products: Clearly define the products you sell, including the type of products, their features, and the target market for each product.

2. Identify suppliers: Identify suppliers who can provide the products you need, taking into consideration factors such as quality, cost, delivery times, and reliability.

3. Develop relationships with suppliers: Build strong relationships with your suppliers by regularly communicating with them, ensuring that they understand your needs and expectations, and working together to resolve any issues.

4. Establish inventory control systems: Establish inventory control systems to help you monitor inventory levels and quickly respond to changes in demand. This may include using barcode scanning, automated inventory management software, or other tools.

5. Monitor inventory levels: Regularly monitor inventory levels to ensure that you always have the right products in stock and to avoid overstocking or stockouts.

6. Manage stockouts: If you experience a stockout, work with your suppliers to quickly replenish your inventory and minimize the impact on your customers.

7. Monitor supply chain performance: Regularly monitor the performance of your supply chain, including delivery times, product quality, and customer satisfaction, to identify areas for improvement.

8. Continuously improve: Continuously evaluate and improve your supply chain to ensure that it remains efficient, effective, and responsive to changing market conditions.

In conclusion, building and managing an effective inventory and supply chain is essential to the success of your business. By defining your products, identifying suppliers, establishing inventory control systems, monitoring inventory levels, and continuously improving your supply chain, you can ensure that you always have the right products in stock, reduce waste, control costs, and improve customer satisfaction.

# Chapter 5: Growing Your Business

## Identifying and Taking Advantage of New Opportunities

As your business grows, it is important to stay aware of new opportunities and continuously evaluate ways to expand and improve your business. Here are some tips to help you identify new opportunities and take advantage of them:

1. Stay informed about your industry - Keeping up-to-date with the latest trends and news in your industry will help you identify new opportunities. Attend trade shows, read industry publications, and join professional organizations to stay informed.

2. Monitor your competition - Study your competition's strengths and weaknesses, and identify areas where you can differentiate yourself or improve on what they are offering.

3. Listen to your customers - Your customers can provide valuable insights into the needs and wants of your target market. Regularly conduct surveys and ask for feedback to help identify new opportunities.

4. Utilize market research - Use market research to identify new opportunities and untapped segments within your target market. This will help you to understand the demand for your products or services, and to make informed decisions about expanding your business.

5. Network and collaborate - Networking and collaboration can open up new opportunities for your business. Attend events and conferences, join professional organizations, and build relationships with other businesses to learn about potential partnerships, joint ventures, and other opportunities.

6. Embrace technology - Technology can provide new opportunities to streamline operations, reach new customers, and improve your products or services. Stay up-to-date with new technology trends, and explore ways to use technology to improve your business.

7. Consider acquisitions or mergers - Consider acquiring or merging with other businesses that complement your own. This can help you expand into new markets, and increase your customer base, products and services offered.

Taking advantage of new opportunities can help you grow your business, increase revenue, and reach new customers. Remember, it is important to be proactive and continuously evaluate opportunities, but it is also important to carefully evaluate the risks and rewards before making a decision. It's important to weigh the potential benefits against the costs and risks involved before making a decision to pursue any new opportunity.

## Utilizing Digital Marketing Strategies to Reach New Customers

The use of digital marketing strategies has become increasingly important for businesses, especially for those starting and operating from home.

With the rise of technology and the widespread use of the internet, it's essential for businesses to have a strong online presence in order to reach and engage with potential customers.

Will provide you with a comprehensive overview of digital marketing strategies and how to effectively implement them to reach new customers.

## Understanding the Basics of Digital Marketing

Digital marketing is a way of promoting and advertising products or services through digital technologies. This includes the use of search engines, websites, social media, email, mobile apps, and other online platforms. The goal of digital marketing is to reach and engage with customers in order to drive sales and growth.

## Developing a Digital Marketing Strategy

Before you can start implementing digital marketing strategies, it's important to develop a comprehensive plan. This should include identifying your target audience, determining the specific channels you want to use, setting goals and objectives, and determining the budget for your campaigns.

## Search Engine Optimization (SEO)

Search engine optimization (SEO) is a critical component of digital marketing. It involves optimizing your website and its content to rank higher in search engine results, making it more visible to potential customers. This can be achieved by using relevant keywords, creating high-quality content, and building backlinks from other websites.

## Social Media Marketing

Social media marketing involves promoting your business through various social media platforms such as Facebook, Instagram, Twitter, LinkedIn, and others.

This can be done by creating a business page, posting engaging content, running ads, and interacting with followers. It's important to choose the right platforms for your business, as not all platforms are suitable for every type of business.

## Email Marketing

Email marketing involves sending marketing messages to a list of subscribers through email. This can be used to promote products and services, share new content, and build relationships with customers. To be effective, emails should be personalized, relevant, and provide value to the recipient.

## Pay-Per-Click Advertising (PPC)

Pay-per-click (PPC) advertising is a form of online advertising where you pay for each click on your ad. This type of advertising can be done through search engines like Google, or through social media platforms like Facebook. PPC advertising can be a quick and effective way to reach a large audience, but it can also be expensive, so it's important to carefully monitor your campaigns to ensure you're getting a positive return on investment.

## Analyzing Results

After you've implemented your digital marketing strategies, it's important to monitor and analyze the results.

This will allow you to see what's working, what's not, and make any necessary changes. Common metrics used to analyze the results of digital marketing campaigns include website traffic, engagement, conversions, and return on investment (ROI).

In conclusion, digital marketing is an essential component of starting and growing a successful business from home. By utilizing the strategies outlined in this chapter, you'll be able to reach and engage with potential customers, drive sales and growth, and ultimately achieve success.

**Expanding your product or service offerings**

Expanding your product or service offerings is a key aspect of growing your business. It is important to be strategic in choosing new offerings so that they complement and enhance your current offerings. When adding new offerings, it is essential to consider the following factors:

1. Market demand: Research your target market to determine what new products or services they are interested in purchasing. Look for any unmet needs that you can address with your new offerings.

2. Competitor analysis: Look at what your competitors are offering and determine if there is an opportunity for you to differentiate your offerings by providing something unique or better.

3. Resource allocation: Consider the resources you will need to bring your new offerings to market, including funding, staffing, and production capabilities.

4. Sales and marketing: Determine the best way to promote and sell your new offerings. This may include updating your website, creating marketing materials, and developing new sales strategies.

When developing your new offerings, it is important to involve your customers in the process. Conduct focus groups or surveys to gather their feedback and make any necessary adjustments. This will help you to ensure that your new offerings meet the needs of your target market and increase your chances of success.

Once you have launched your new offerings, it is important to track their performance. Analyze sales data and customer feedback to determine which offerings are most popular and make any necessary adjustments. This will help you to continue to grow your business and achieve long-term success.

Expanding your customer base by targeting new market segments Establishing strategic partnerships and collaborations to reach new customers and markets Investing in research and development to continuously improve your products or services

Developing and executing a comprehensive marketing plan to raise awareness of your brand and drive sales Improving customer service and experience to increase customer loyalty and referrals Staying on top of industry trends and adapting to changes in the market to stay relevant and competitive.

It is important to remember that growing your business is not just about increasing sales and profits, but also about continuously improving and evolving to meet the changing needs of your customers and the market.

To achieve sustainable growth, you need to have a clear understanding of your target market and competition, and develop strategies to differentiate yourself and stand out in a crowded market.

To take advantage of new opportunities, you need to be proactive and constantly on the lookout for new trends, technologies, and market shifts. You can do this by conducting market research, staying informed about industry developments, and networking with other business owners and professionals in your industry.

Digital marketing strategies can be a powerful tool for reaching new customers and expanding your customer base. With the rise of e-commerce and the widespread use of technology, there are many opportunities to reach potential customers through online channels, such as social media, email marketing, search engine optimization, and online advertising.

By incorporating digital marketing strategies into your overall marketing plan, you can reach a wider audience and target specific market segments more effectively. It is important to develop a well-rounded digital marketing strategy that leverages multiple channels and incorporates various tactics to reach your target audience and drive conversions.

Expanding your product or service offerings can also be an effective way to grow your business. This can involve introducing new products or services that complement your existing offerings, or diversifying into new markets or industries. When considering expanding your offerings, it is important to conduct market research to ensure that there is demand for your new products or services and that they align with your overall business strategy.

In conclusion, growing your business requires a combination of strategy, planning, and execution. By taking advantage of new opportunities, leveraging digital marketing strategies, expanding your offerings, and continuously improving and adapting to changes in the market, you can create a successful and sustainable business that will thrive for years to come.

## Building and maintaining relationships with customers, suppliers, and partners

Building and maintaining strong relationships with customers, suppliers, and partners is an important part of growing and sustaining a successful business. These relationships form the foundation of your business and are crucial for its success in the long-term. In this chapter, we'll discuss the strategies and best practices for building and maintaining strong relationships with key stakeholders.

The first step in building strong relationships with customers is to understand their needs and wants. This can be done through regular customer surveys, focus groups, and market research. By understanding your customers, you can tailor your products and services to meet their needs and create a stronger connection with them. Additionally, you should also be responsive to customer complaints and feedback and take steps to address their concerns in a timely manner.

It is also important to build strong relationships with suppliers. A reliable supplier can make or break your business, so it is essential to find one that you can trust. When searching for suppliers, it is important to consider factors such as quality, price, delivery times, and customer service. Once you have found a supplier that meets your needs, it is important to develop a strong relationship with them by communicating regularly, paying bills on time, and providing constructive feedback.

Partnerships are another important aspect of growing your business. Partnerships can provide access to new customers, new markets, and new technologies. When searching for a partner, it is important to consider factors such as compatibility, strengths, weaknesses, and goals. Additionally, it is important to have clear, concise agreements in place to ensure a smooth working relationship.

Finally, it is important to maintain strong relationships with all key stakeholders. This can be done by staying in touch with customers, suppliers, and partners on a regular basis, acknowledging their contributions, and being honest and transparent in all communications. Additionally, it is important to be proactive in addressing any issues that may arise and to resolve conflicts in a constructive and timely manner.

In conclusion, building and maintaining strong relationships with customers, suppliers, and partners is crucial for the success of any business. By understanding the needs of your stakeholders, being responsive to their concerns, and maintaining open and honest communication, you can build relationships that will last for many years to come.

# Conclusion:

Starting a successful business from home requires a lot of hard work and dedication. From assessing your business idea and conducting market research, to setting up your business and building and managing your online presence, every step of the process requires careful consideration and attention to detail.

It is also important to remember that success does not happen overnight. Growing your business takes time, effort, and patience, but with a solid plan in place and a commitment to continuously learning and improving, you can turn your business into a thriving and profitable enterprise.

In this book, we have covered some of the key aspects of starting and running a successful business from home, but there is always more to learn and explore. Whether you are just starting out or have been in business for a while, always keep an eye out for new opportunities and be open to trying new strategies to grow and improve your business.

Remember, the most important ingredient for success is passion and determination. With these qualities and the right guidance, you can turn your dream of running a successful business from home into a reality.

In conclusion, starting a successful business from home is an achievable goal for anyone with the drive, passion, and the right plan in place. By taking the time to assess your business idea, create a solid business plan, set up your business, build and manage your online presence, and grow your business over time, you can achieve your entrepreneurial dreams and build a thriving business.

Remember that success in business doesn't happen overnight. It takes time, effort, and persistence. But with a well-planned strategy and a focus on your goals, you can turn your business into a success story. Don't be afraid to take risks, pivot when necessary, and never stop learning and growing.

Starting a business from home can be a fulfilling and exciting journey. So take the leap, trust in yourself, and let's get started on building a successful business today!

www.ingramcontent.com/pod-product-compliance
Lightning Source LLC
Chambersburg PA
CBHW050308220526
45465CB00002B/870